GUIDE TO

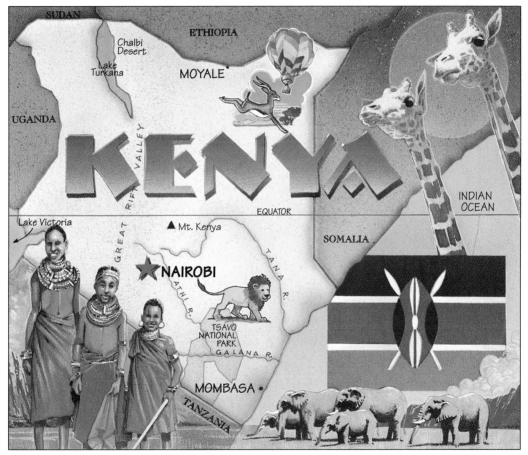

DAVID MARSHALL

Highlights for Children

CONTENTS

On the cover: Giraffes in Kenya's Tsavo National Park
with Mt. Kilimanjaro (in neighboring Tanzania) in
the background

Published by Highlights for Children
© 1996 Highlights for Children, Inc.
P.O. Box 18201
Columbus, Ohio 43218-0201

10 9 8 7 6 5 4 3
ISBN 0-87534-920-X

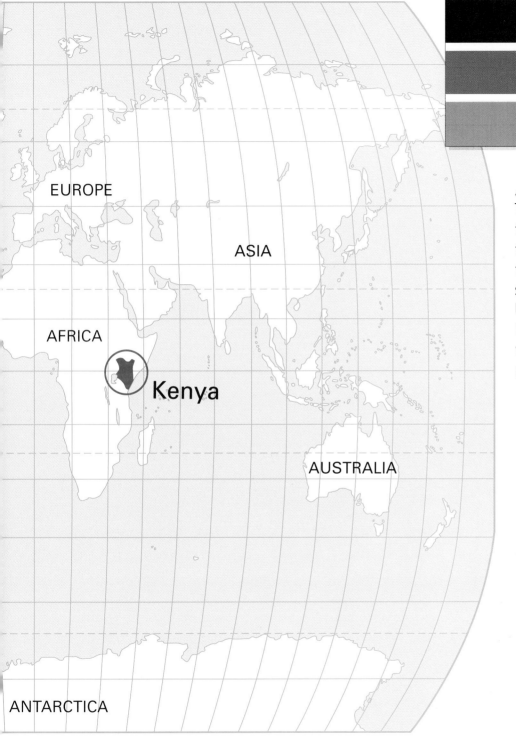

EUROPE

ASIA

AFRICA

Kenya

AUSTRALIA

ANTARCTICA

△ **The Kenyan flag**
The shield and the
three colors represent
the country's fight for
freedom. Black is for
skin color, red is for
blood shed, and green
is for the country. The
white stripes are for
peace.

3

KENYA AT A GLANCE

Area 225,100 square miles (583,000 square kilometers)

Population 27,000,000

Capital Nairobi, population more than 1,900,000

Other large cities Mombasa (population 550,000), Kisumu (225,000)

Highest mountain Mt. Kenya, 17,057 feet (5,199 meters)

Longest river Tana, 443 miles (708 kilometers)

Largest lake Lake Turkana, 2,473 square miles (6,405 square kilometers) Lake Victoria is bigger, but only part of it lies within Kenya.

Official language KiSwahili

▽ **Kenyan stamps** They show examples of Kenya's wildlife, Olympic success, and projects designed to help the poor.

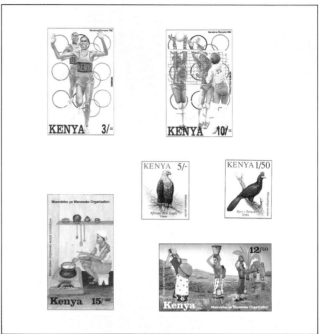

◁ **Kenyan money** The unit of currency is the Kenya shilling (KSh). The KSh 20 bill features the current president of the Republic of Kenya, Daniel arap Moi, on one side, and the Moi International Sports Center, Kasarani, in Nairobi, on the other.

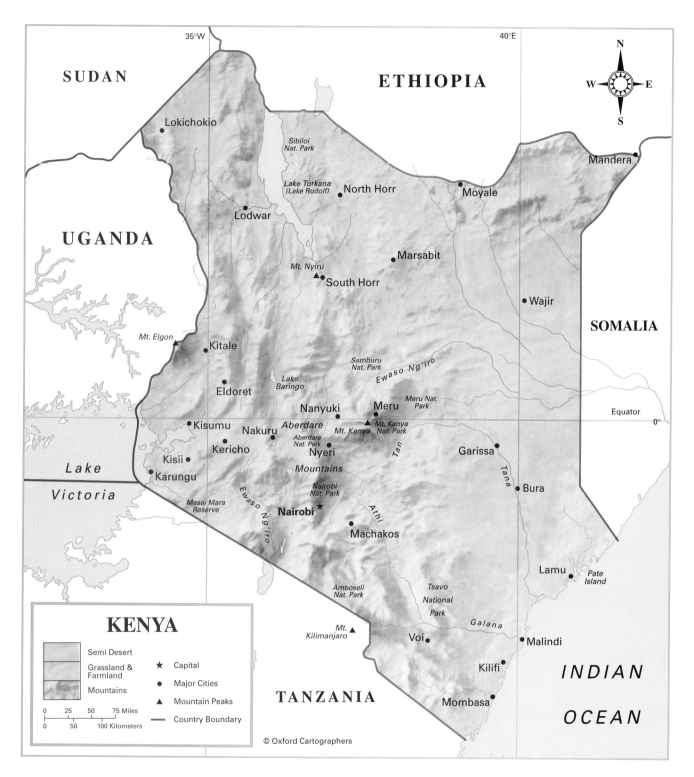

SUDAN

ETHIOPIA

35°W

40°E

N
W E
S

Lokichokio

Sibiloi
Nat. Park

Lake Turkana
(Lake Rudolf)

North Horr

Moyale

Mandera

Lodwar

UGANDA

Marsabit

Mt. Nyiru
South Horr

Wajir

SOMALIA

Mt. Elgon

Kitale

Samburu
Nat. Park

Ewaso Ng'iro

Eldoret

Lake
Baringo

Nanyuki

Meru

Meru Nat.
Park

Equator

0°

Kisumu

Nakuru

Aberdare

Aberdare
Nat. Park

Mt. Kenya
Mt. Kenya
Nat. Park

Tana

Garissa

Kericho

Nyeri

Kisii

Karungu

Mountains

Nairobi
Nat. Park

Tana

Bura

Lake

Masai Mara
Reserve

Ewaso Ng'iro

Nairobi ★

Athi

Victoria

Machakos

Lamu

Pate
Island

Amboseli
Nat. Park

Tsavo
National
Park

Galana

Voi

Malindi

Mt.
Kilimanjaro

Kilifi

KENYA

TANZANIA

Mombasa

INDIAN

OCEAN

Semi Desert

Grassland &
Farmland

Mountains

0   25   50   75 Miles

0   50   100 Kilometers

★ Capital

● Major Cities

▲ Mountain Peaks

— Country Boundary

© Oxford Cartographers

5

A MIX OF PEOPLE AND WILDLIFE

Kenya is a country in eastern Africa. It is a large country, almost as big as Texas. It is nearly surrounded by five other African countries — Ethiopia, Tanzania, Somalia, Sudan, and Uganda. The Indian Ocean washes against the coast in the southeast.

The land is quite different from one region to the next. There is rich farmland and forest, dry scrubland, semi-deserts, mangrove swamps, and coral reefs. Africa's Great Rift Valley runs north and south through the country. In Kenya alone, this huge trench is 50 miles (80 kilometers) wide, 375 miles (600 kilometers) long, and 2,000 feet (600 meters) deep.

The earth's equator crosses the center of Kenya. Much of the country is hot, but it is warm along the coast and cool in the highlands. In fact, the peaks of Mt. Kenya are covered with snow all year round!

△ **Samburu girl in traditional costume** The Samburu people wear brightly colored clothes, headbands, and jewelry.

Most Kenyans are of African origin. There are more than forty ethnic groups recognized in the country. People from Arab, Asian, and European backgrounds live here, too. So there is a mixture of cultures in Kenya today. KiSwahili, the main African language, has many Arab words in it. Most people are Christians, but there is also a large Muslim community. Eight out of ten Kenyans earn their living by farming.

To people from other countries, Kenya is probably most famous for its wildlife. Many rare animals live in its national parks and wildlife reserves. These include Africa's plains animals, such as elephants, giraffes, zebras, rhinoceros, cheetahs, and lions. People come from all over the world to go on safari here. But the animal and plant life is only one of the many fascinating things to see. Welcome to Kenya!

◁ **Elephants cool off in the Uaso Nyiro River** Females look after the young elephants and, in the distance, an adult male looks on.

▷ **Coffee workers, Kiambu Kenya** Coffee and tea are Kenya's most important crops. After they pick the coffee beans, workers separate them by hand.

THE COMMERCIAL CROSSROADS

Nairobi is Kenya's capital city. It is also the country's thriving business and industrial center. Today nearly two million people live there. Nairobi is a major "crossroads" area — the Great North Road runs between Cape Town in South Africa and Cairo in Egypt. And the Trans-Africa Highway runs from Mombasa to Lagos in Nigeria. Nairobi is a

▽ **The Jamia Mosque** This Muslim place of worship is highly ornate on the outside, but inside it is very plain and simple.

center of air travel, too. Airplanes from about thirty companies use the Jomo Kenyatta International Airport.

The area was an important source of water for the Masai tribe until the Kenya-Uganda railway was built. Nairobi Railway Station is in the heart of the city. At the Railway Museum you can climb inside some early locomotives and look back in time through the city's history.

On Parliament Road you will see the government buildings. You can often get a permit to enter the public gallery, where you can watch what goes on inside. Farther along Parliament Road is the burial place of President Jomo Kenyatta, who was Kenya's first president. Kenyatta worked very hard to get independent rule for Kenya. Many buildings are named after him, including the huge Kenyatta International Conference Center. The beautiful domes of the Jamia Mosque are a marvelous sight. Try to see them at night, when they are lit up.

Food comes from a variety of cultures. Two popular local dishes are *ugali* (a stiff porridge made from corn flour) and *nyama choma* (barbecued goat meat or beef). You can also enjoy Asian cooking and even fish and chips or burgers!

The best place to shop for souvenirs is the City Market in the center of Nairobi. All kinds of local crafts are on display. Many are fascinating and inexpensive.

◁ **A typical market stall** Here you will find baskets, embroidered cloths, and carvings made from ebony and soapstone.

▽ **View over Nairobi** In this view from the top of the Kenyatta Conference Center, Nairobi's tallest building, you can see in the foreground Holy Family Minor Basilica (left) and City Hall (right).

OUTSIDE THE CITY

Nairobi provides a home for a great many animals as well as for people. It is just a short bus or taxi ride from the center of the city to Nairobi National Park. Gazelle, lions, zebras, giraffes, and rhinoceros live here. There is a permanent water supply in the park, so if you visit in a dry season, there will be even more animals to see.

There is also an animal orphanage where sick or injured animals can be nursed until they are ready to return to the wild. Another place to see some of the animals up close, and even feed them, is at the Langata Giraffe Center.

Life in the center of Nairobi looks at first like life in any other big city, but you do not have to travel far to see tribal customs here. Try visiting the Bomas of Kenya, a village made up of traditional homesteads.

Kenyans are especially talented in sports that involve running. Kipchoge Keino was the first Olympic gold medal winner from Kenya. Since the 1960s, Kenyans have established themselves as champion middle-distance and long-distance runners. The Moi International Sports Center, Kasarani, is the site of many important sporting events. It is also a major training center for Kenya's Olympic-bound athletes.

The famous writer Karen Blixen lived near Nairobi. Her book *Out of Africa*, which was made into a movie, told the story of life on her farm. Today you can visit the Karen Blixen Museum, 10 miles (16 kilometers) south of Nairobi. It is in the house where she lived. Everything on display tells visitors about her time there, which began in 1917. You can see the Ngong Hills from the house. If you climb them, the view you have of Nairobi is the same view that Karen Blixen enjoyed. It will give you a good way to get one last look at Kenya's capital.

△ **The Bomas of Kenya** At this traditional village built around the cultural center at Langata, you can watch dancers and singers from different tribes.

▷ **The Ngong Hills** Early settlers cut out farms on the slopes of the Ngong Hills. Today these are good places to see the hilltops, or to admire the view of Nairobi down into the Rift Valley.

▽ **The Langata Giraffe Center** Tourists climb up on special wooden platforms to feed the animals.

WEST TO LAKE VICTORIA

More people live in the western part of Kenya than in Nairobi. They are mainly farmers. Some of the best roads in Kenya are in this region, so it is easy to travel around by bus. But you might choose to ride in a *matatu*. This vehicle, typical of Kenya, is a small bus or van, often owned by the driver. Its name comes from the KiSwahili word meaning "three," because the fare to ride in a matatu around Nairobi used to be three cents.

Lake Victoria forms part of Kenya's western border with Uganda and Tanzania. Its shores are the home of the Luo people, the third-largest tribal group in Kenya. They have traditionally been fishermen, but many now live in towns.

Fishing boats sail from the villages on the southeastern shore. A few of the boats have lateen, or triangular, sails. This type of sail was copied from Arab ships. You can go out in a fishing boat to try to catch a Giant Nile Perch. You can also sail to the quiet island of Mfangano. At Hippo Point the views across the lake are beautiful, and if you are patient you may see hippos splashing around in the water.

Up in the cool western highlands is Kericho, Kenya's tea capital. Tea is Kenya's second most valuable crop after coffee. The land in the area is also very good for growing wheat and potatoes.

The Gusii people live farther up in the highlands. Tabaka village is the best place to see their soapstone quarries and sculptures.

The Kakamega forest, a small patch of jungle in the west, shows another side of Kenya's mixed scenery. It is home to many rare reptiles and birds, and so it is of great interest to conservationists.

▷ **Mfangano Island** On this small island there are many ancient rock paintings to see.

12

◁ **A crowded bus near Nairobi** Buses are Kenya's cheapest and most popular form of transportation.

▽ **Tea picking in the highlands around Kericho** Most work on plantations is still done by hand, not by machines.

THE GREAT RIFT VALLEY

Most of Kenya's lakes along the African Rift Valley lie in the craters of old volcanoes. The water is very salty, even though the lakes are many miles from the sea. Deposits of salt and other minerals build up in them because the water does not flow in and out in rivers, but arrives as rain and leaves as water vapor. Lake Magadi is the most salty of all. Hot springs carrying lots of salt pour out of the ground and into this lake. As the sun and wind dry the lake out, the salt is left behind. The Kenyans collect the salt and other minerals and sell them.

Lake Naivasha is different from the others because it is a freshwater lake. This is a puzzle to scientists; they do not know how or where the water flows out of it to carry the salt away. The volcanic land around this lake is very good for growing crops. Tons of vegetables, fruits, and flowers are harvested every year to sell in Nairobi. Lake Naivasha is also a wonderful place for birdwatching.

Lake Nakuru is another saltwater lake. Flamingos gather there to eat, and so the area has been made a national park. It also now has a rhinoceros sanctuary.

◁ **The Eastern Slope of the Great Rift Valley** The Rift Valley is a giant ditch 3,125 miles (5,000 kilometers) long. It runs through Kenya and much of eastern Africa. This view is from Lasiolo, Mt. Maralal.

▷ **Flamingos at Lake Nakuru** The birds love to eat the blue-green algae that grow on the lake's surface.

▷ **Soapstone carvings** These figures are popular souvenirs. The soft stone is gathered from a quarry and then hand carved.

The Mt. Elgon National Park is one of the best places to see elephants. They particularly like to visit Kitum Cave. The walls of the cave are salty. Elephants need salt in their diet, and over years of licking they have managed to dig tunnels reaching far into the mountainside!

Take a matatu from the town of Kitale, best known for its blue gum trees, to the nearby Saiwa Swamp. Here you may spot the rare sitatunga antelope and the black-and-white colobus monkey. The area is their protected habitat.

FROM FIELD STUDIES TO FOSSILS

The Marich Pass Field Studies Center in Kenya's northwest is the starting point if you are going on safari with English-speaking Turkana or Pokot guides. Turkana men traditionally cover part of their hair with mud, which is then painted blue and decorated with ostrich and other feathers. The guides will take you on a tour of this small wildlife sanctuary. Animals such as baboons, antelopes, elephants, and wart-hogs live here.

Beyond the Marich Pass itself lie the desert plains. After leaving the Marich Pass, turn left and you will arrive at the Turkwel Gorge hydroelectric project. Part of the plan is to build the highest dam of its kind in Africa. The work has been done with great care to protect the gorge from damage. When it is completely finished, the lake will be used for all sorts of water sports.

Lake Turkana is the largest lake in Kenya. It is at the center of a wide group of national parks. The world's largest colony of Nile crocodiles lives in the lake. You may see them sliding into the water from Central Island, an old volcano in the lake.

▽ **Turkana elder on way to nearest water supply** Gourds, the dried rinds of large fruit, are used to carry water.

▽ **Fossils at Koobi Fora, at the edge of Lake Turkana** A guide shows visitors two-million-year-old fossilized elephant bones.

△ **Traditional Turkana dress** Despite the heat, the elders of the tribe usually wear a woolen blanket.

The town of Lodwar, to the west, is a lively place centered around a busy market. Turkana people can be seen making and selling their goods there. You can take a ride to Lake Turkana from Lodwar, but before you set out, make sure the wind is not too strong. The west coast of the lake is often blasted by very fierce gales.

Boat trips are popular for fishing or to visit Koobi Fora. Here, in the 1970s, fossil-hunter Richard Leakey found pieces of a skull that once belonged to an ancestor of humans. Two people worked for six weeks to put the pieces of the skull together. Their work showed that the first humans were alive earlier than anyone had ever thought.

THE GIANT OF KENYA

Mt. Kenya, the second-tallest mountain in all of Africa, is an extinct volcano. As you climb to the top you will see surprising changes in the landscape. The lower slopes are farmed by the Kikuyu, Kenya's largest tribal group. There they produce a large amount of Kenya's food. The ground is very good because of the rivers and the rich lava soil. Above this area, there is a strip of rain forest where elephants, buffalo, and rhinoceros roam. Higher still, heather and other small flowering plants grow. At 15,000 feet (4,500 meters) you might see antelope or zebras. The peaks are covered with snow.

The lovely mountain is not the only spectacular sight in this area. The scenery around the town of Nyahururu is beautiful. The best way to see it is to travel there by road from Nakuru. The waterfalls here are known as "T. Falls" after Joseph Thomson, a Scottish explorer of the 1880s. Thomson was the first European to walk from Mombasa to Lake Victoria.

Traveling northeast from T. Falls, you come to Isiolo. Beyond this small frontier town is an enormous region of semi-deserts and scrubland. The area is very lively. A variety of tribal peoples lives here, including the Samburu, the Rendille, the Boran, and the Turkana.

Isiolo lies between two national parks. To the south is the Meru National Park, where naturalists Joy and George Adamson's famous lioness Elsa was returned to the wild. The Samburu Park, to the northeast of Isiolo, is the home of the Grevy zebra and the Somali ostrich. The gerenuk antelope also lives here. This animal is remarkable because it travels on its hind legs.

▽ **Boran girls in traditional dress** The Boran people roam northern Kenya — always seeking water and grazing land for their cattle.

◁ **A camel trek across Samburu National Park** Local tribesmen lead the tourists on safari.

▽ **The summit of Mt. Kenya** Tourists who climb the mountain will see snow and glaciers at the equator at any time of year.

BALLOON SAFARI!

Most people agree that the Masai Mara Game Reserve is the most beautiful of Kenya's wildlife parks. It joins the Serengeti National Park in Tanzania. You can see the animals crossing between the two countries — they are not worried by borders. They make a wonderful sight, especially the huge herds of wildebeests that cross to Kenya in summer and back to Tanzania in October.

▽ **Masai woman and baby** She is singing to welcome guests to their village on the Masai Mara.

Hippos and crocodiles swim in the Mara River. Large numbers of land animals — from lions to the dik-dik, a tiny antelope — roam freely.

The Masai tribe still lives on part of the parkland. Their villages are just outside the park. Thousands of tourists come here with cameras. The Masai people will often find the time to talk to visitors.

The best way to see the park is by hot-air balloon. Taking off soon after dawn, the balloon gives you great views of the animals and the savannah plains.

Just to the southeast is the Amboseli National Park. On the border with Tanzania, Mt. Kilimanjaro rises in the background. This is another popular place for tourists and photographers. The Amboseli Lake is sometimes completely dry.

The Tsavo National Park, the largest wildlife reserve in Kenya, is located between Amboseli and Malindi. The bush country is dusty and rocky but interesting to explore. At the Mzima Springs, hippos and crocodiles swim into view from an underwater passage. Follow the nature trails to Mt. Shetani to explore the caves there and learn about this volcano's lava flows.

▷ **Hot-air balloon ride** This is an exciting way to watch the wild animals without disturbing them.

◁ **A lioness with her cubs in the Masai Mara Game Reserve** They spend most of the day lying under the bushes or stretched out in the sun.

IN AND AROUND MOMBASA

Mombasa is Kenya's second-largest urban center. It is linked by a railroad to Nairobi and Lake Victoria. The history of Mombasa goes back to the 1300s when it was founded as a trading port. Parts of the old town are still standing and are well worth exploring. Some of the houses are made from wattle and daub and coral rag. You can also see the finely carved doors and shutters that are typical of Swahili buildings. The word "Swahili" comes from *sahel,* the Arabic word for coast, but is now used for almost any Muslim who lives on the coast. Before the Arabs arrived, the Africans of this region were the Bajun and the Shinozi peoples.

The history of Fort Jesus, on Mombasa Island, tells clearly how Mombasa has had many different rulers over the years. Built by Portuguese colonists in 1593, it was conquered nine times between 1631 and 1875. It is now a museum where many historical objects are on display.

Parts of the southern coast are very popular vacation resorts. Diani, to the south of Mombasa, has white sandy beaches, very clear blue water, and coconut palms. There is a lot of underwater life to see here, including shoals of angel, zebra, and parrot fish. But you may prefer simply to relax and enjoy the swimming and watersports.

There is also a wide choice of restaurants catering to visitors from around the world. Swahili dishes, made with coconuts and coconut milk, are the local specialty.

The market is a good place to shop for *makonde* wood carvings, such as chess sets or animals. You can also find *khangas*, colorful, patterned pieces of cloth for wraparound skirts, often with Swahili proverbs embroidered on them.

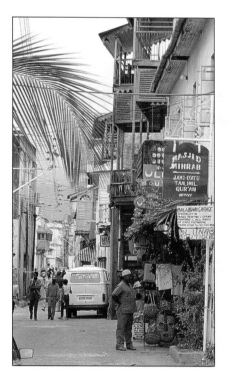

▷ **Mombasa Old Town** Mombasa is the largest port on the coast of East Africa, with a population of nearly 550,000. Much of the old town still stands.

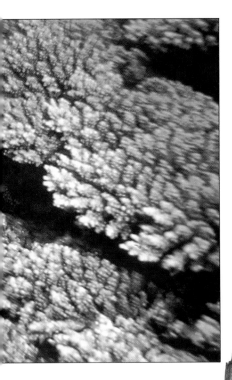

◁ **Colorful fish off Kenya's south coast** Tourists can take glass-bottomed boats from Mombasa to see the underwater life.

▽ **Fort Jesus, Mombasa** The fort was a stronghold for Portuguese colonists until they were forced by Arabs to leave Kenya in 1720.

23

THE NORTH COAST

From Mombasa, you can travel by road to the northern coast of Kenya. But it is much more fun to sail there in a *dhow*, a wooden dugout boat with triangular sails. In the north, the sails are made at Shela village.

The town of Malindi is now a popular vacation resort, but it also has a fascinating history. The Portuguese explorer Vasco da Gama landed here in 1498. A pillar that he put up to help sailors set their course still stands at the southern end of the bay.

Tiger sharks, hammerhead sharks, and barracuda can sometimes be seen from boats in the Marine National Park. Or you may prefer to scuba dive or swim in the calm of the coral gardens. The pillar of pink rock called Hell's Kitchen is one of the most interesting sights on the coast. The rock is so worn away that you can walk through and see how it was formed.

Lamu, a lovely island just off the coast, is the location of Kenya's oldest port — also called Lamu. In the port's residential area, the carved doors of the houses are more than 1,000 years old. There are displays of Lamu's history in the Omani Fort. In the 1800s this building was a prison. The Pwani Mosque was built in Lamu in the late 1300s. The port is still important for Muslims. They can be seen wearing the traditional dress of *bui bui*, a long black robe for women, and *khanzu*, a white suit for men.

The other islands nearby have many historical sites and can be reached by dhow or by motorboat. On Manda Island are the remains of an old Swahili town at Takwa. People still live on Paté Island. Most of them are fishermen and mangrove pole cutters.

◁ **Carving wood in Lamu** As you walk through the town, you will see beautifully carved doors and shutters.

◁ **Swimming pool at the Sinbad Hotel, Malindi** To the north of Malindi there are miles of sandy beaches and dunes.

▽ **Sailing past Omani Fort** The fort overlooks the Lamu waterfront. There are more boats on this part of the coast than anywhere else on the East African coast.

NORTH OF THE TANA

Garissa and Wajir are the two main towns in the northeast. There is little to do in Garissa, but the nearby Tana River Reserve is the last sanctuary of colobus and mangabey monkeys. Wajir has a lively market and is an interesting town. Many of the buildings are white with small towers on top.

To the north, on the Ethiopian border, is Moyale. Some houses here have mud-and-stick roofs that are about 5 feet (150 centimeters) thick and held up by poles. You might expect them to fall down, but chickens and goats walk around on them. They are stronger than they look.

▷ **Maralal town** The name means "glittering" in Samburu. It comes from the gleaming corrugated iron roof of the first modern building in the town.

In the town of Loyangalani you will see houses made from stick and doum-palm leaves. Here the Turkana tribe lives side by side with the El-Molo people. The Turkana are known as skillful herdsmen and brave watchmen.

Most of northern Kenya is desertlike. You will want to visit the towns of Marsabit and Maikona on the edge of the Chalbi Desert, the only real desert in Kenya. The Rendille people live in Marsabit and are famous for their elaborate braided hair and beaded necklaces and bracelets. They may not stay here for long periods of time as many are camel herders who are used to roaming across the deserts.

The Samburu people live in Maralal. This town is a bit like the American wild west used to be. The streets are very dusty and the big covered porches of the houses jut out into them. Samburu guides will take you on camel safaris in the region — a marvelous way to end your journey around the fascinating country of Kenya.

◁ **Samburu warriors watching over their cattle near Maralal** Often Samburu men are warriors until they are over thirty years old. After this they become elders and can marry.

▷ **Gabbra woman making a basket** The Gabbra tribe is one of several to live in the towns on the edge of the Chalbi desert.

KENYA FACTS AND FIGURES

People

Kenya has a population of around 27 million. The great majority are Africans. Tribal groupings make up 90% of the total African population. The Kikuyu, the Masai, the Luhya, the Luo, and the Turkana tribes are the largest. Around 800,000 Asians, 40,000 Arabs, and 40,000 Europeans also live in Kenya.

Trade and Industry

Tourism and coffee are the main industries in Kenya.

Most manufacturing is centered around Nairobi and Mombasa. The main products are processed foods, building materials, glass, chemicals, and car assembly.

Kenya also exports soda ash and fluorspar, used to make steel, although mining is a very small part of the economy. Many of the available minerals, including silver, gold, lead, and limestone, have not been mined commercially.

Kenya has to buy sources of energy, particularly oil from Saudi Arabia. The hydroelectric projects now being built mean that Kenya will soon be able to generate most of its own energy.

△ **Kikuyu tribespeople in traditional dress** Here they are entertaining the tourists.

Farming

Agriculture employs about eight out of every ten of the Kenyan population and supplies at least half of the products Kenya sells abroad. Food crops include maize (corn), beans, and fruit. The main money-earning crops are coffee, tea, and cotton fibers.

About 17% of the land in Kenya is good for farming. This includes the southern slopes of Mt. Kenya, cultivated by the Kikuyu people, and the rich volcanic soil around Lake Naivasha, ideal for growing fruits and vegetables.

Cattle and sheep are raised in a few areas of Kenya.

Fishing

Fishing is not as important as it used to be in Kenya. The fishing fleets of Lake Victoria and the coastal fishermen of the Bajun, Swahili, Shirazi, and Bantu tribes supply most of the fish the country needs for use by its own people.

Food

The African tribes have their own traditional foods, and you will find that local dishes vary from region to region. Also, many of the peoples who invaded Kenya over the years brought new foods and styles of cooking. For example, the Portuguese brought oranges and lemons in the 15th century.

Swahili food often includes coconut milk because the tribe lives on the south coast near the coconut palms. *Kaimati* is a Swahili doughnut. Other specialties include *mkate myai* (egg and minced meat flapjacks) and *Sukuma Wiki,* a popular vegetable dish. A great deal of maize is grown in Kenya, so *ugali,* a thick porridge made from corn flour, is common. In large towns there are usually restaurants selling Asian and European dishes.

Schools

Kenyan children start school around the age of six. Normally, they go to primary school for eight years. Many children drop out of education before they reach secondary school age, but this number is getting smaller. After secondary school, students can go on to university if they meet all the requirements.

The Media

Television ownership is widespread among Kenyans, particularly in Nairobi and Mombasa. Most TV programs in Kenya are bought from the United States and Europe. The Kenya Broadcasting Corporation broadcasts in English, KiSwahili, and other African languages. The British Broadcasting Corporation's World Service also transmits to Kenya each day, again in both English and KiSwahili. Voice of America is also received in Kenya.

Newspapers are available in either language. *The Daily Nation*, *The Kenya Times*, and *The Standard* are published in English. *Taifa Leo* is published in KiSwahili. There are also many magazines.

△ **Meru woman at her roadside vegetable stand** Buses traveling long distances stop at such places to let passengers buy something to eat or drink.

Religion

Various religions are practiced in Kenya. Christianity is the most widespread, although Muslims make up about 30% of Kenya's population. There are Hindu temples across Kenya, and many tribal groups have kept their own beliefs and customs.

Sports

Kenyan middle-distance runners are the best in the world. The number of medals they won between 1964 and 1984 is amazing. Kenyan athletes won seventeen Olympic track medals, even though politics prevented them from taking part in the Games in 1976 and 1980. The list of great runners includes Henry Rono and Kipchoge Keino.

Soccer, called football, is played by almost all Kenyans, using any available piece of flat ground. The Kenyan national team, the Harambee Stars, won the East and Central Africa Challenge Cup between 1981 and 1983. European soccer teams often visit Kenya playing on tours.

Volleyball is also popular. It is played in schools and by adults in club teams around the country. Like soccer and volleyball, cricket is enjoyed by players and spectators.

Watersports, such as snorkeling and windsurfing, are enjoyed at the many coastal resorts and clubs, especially by tourists.

The Safari Rally is an important international event. Every year at Easter, drivers from all over the world arrive in Nairobi and then race across Kenya in their cars. The event was founded to celebrate the Coronation of Queen Elizabeth II in 1953 and now attracts top drivers and television coverage, too.

KENYA FACTS AND FIGURES

Festivals and Holidays

Most holidays in Kenya are connected to religious, political, or historical events. They include:

April **Easter**
May 1 **Labor Day**
June 1 **Madaraka Day**
Commemorates the first elected government
October 10 **Moi Day**
Anniversary of President Moi's inauguration
October 20 **Kenyatta Day** Honors Jomo Kenyatta, Kenya's first president, on the day he was arrested in 1952 by British colonists in Kenya's struggle for independence
December 12 **Jamhuri** Kenya's Independence Day
December 25 **Christmas Day**
'Id al-Fitr, a Muslim holiday, is also celebrated. It marks the first sighting of the new moon, so the date changes each year.

The Arts

Examples of Kenyan art include soapstone sculptures, made in the villages around Kisii in the west, and *Makonde* carvings made from ebony. Batik paintings are also very interesting, as scenes and people are recorded in tiny detail by using hot wax on good silk.

△ **A farming settlement in western Kenya**
The large farms of early colonists have been divided up and given out to local African communities, as here.

Beaded jewelry, such as that made by the Masai tribe, is very striking. You can buy necklaces, anklets, wristbands, and earrings.

The Nairobi Music Society encourages local musicians and supports the Nairobi Orchestra, which is well known and popular throughout Africa.

There are also several good theaters in the capital, including the National Theater and the Braeburn Theater, which stage a mixture of traditional and modern performances.

Plants

Because of Kenya's varied climate, a huge range of plant life can be found. In the south, low, wide acacia trees—also called thorn trees for their prickly branches—are common, as are bottle-shaped baobab trees and thornbushes.

On Mt. Kenya you will find practically every kind of plant life imaginable. In the north of Kenya there is a combination of desert bush and scrubland. Mangrove and palm trees grow on the coast.

Animals

Many people visit Kenya just to see all the animals. Lions, buffalos, wildebeests, elephants, leopards, rhinoceros, gazelles, warthogs, cheetahs, hyenas, and antelopes are only some of the land animals to be found in the large number of Kenya's national parks. There are insects and spiders everywhere.

There is an equal variety of bird life, including flamingos, storks, ostriches, eagles, vultures, owls, parrots, and pelicans. Crocodiles and hippos are common in the lakes and rivers. Marine life includes angel and zebra fish.

30

HISTORY

The first group of settlers in Kenya arrived about 6,000 years ago from Ethiopia. The Bantu people from western Africa and the Nilotic herdsmen from Sudan followed about 2,000 years later. This explains the many variations among Kenya's tribal peoples.

Coastal Kenya became home to Arabs and Persians. These settlers intermarried with the locals, leading to the evolution of the Swahili people, who have a largely Islamic culture. They built towns such as Mombasa, Malindi, and Lamu along the coast. In the 1800s they journeyed all the way to Lake Victoria but were not welcomed by the tribes.

The European colonists then moved into much of Africa, and Kenya was ruled by Britons from 1895. This was unpopular with the tribal peoples, who wished to rule themselves.

The Europeans brought the Kenyan economy up to date, particularly in the areas of agriculture and communications. But the Kikuyu people, who were most affected by these new uses of the land, were unhappy about it. Their unrest led to action. It began with the first Kikuyu political organizations in the 1920s and ended in 1963 when the Mau Mau rebellion won Kenya's independence from Great Britain. Jomo Kenyatta, the rebel leader, became the country's first president.

Not all has gone smoothly since independence, but the country's economy is reasonably healthy. The country has been enjoying a period of stability under President Daniel arap Moi.

LANGUAGE

The official languages in Kenya are KiSwahili and English. There are also many tribal languages spoken across the country. The major ones are Kikuyu, Luo, and Luhya. Many tribal people have learned KiSwahili in order to speak to one another, so it is the most useful language for visitors to know.

Useful words and phrases

English	KiSwahili
one	moja
two	mbili
three	tatu

Useful words and phrases

English	KiSwahili
four	nne
five	tano
six	sita
seven	saba
eight	nane
nine	tisa
ten	kumi
Saturday	jumamosi
Sunday	jumapili
Monday	jumatatu
Tuesday	jumanne
Wednesday	jumatano
Thursday	alhamisi
Friday	ijumaa

Useful words and phrases

English	KiSwahili
Hello	jambo or habari
Good-bye	kwaheri
yes	ndiyo
no	hapana or la
Thank you	asante
What's your name?	unaitwa nani?
How are you?	habari?
today	leo
tomorrow	kesho
eat	kula
sleep	lala
food	chakula
water	maji

INDEX

Note: Many Kenyan words have more than one spelling—for example, KiSwahili and Kiswahili, Masai and Maasai, Chalbi and Chilba, and other names of places, tribes, and especially foods.

Book created for Highlights for Children, Inc.
by Bender Richardson White.
Editors: Peter MacDonald and Lionel Bender
Designer: Malcolm Smythe
Art Editor: Ben White
Editorial Assistant: Madeleine Samuel
Picture Researcher: Annabel Ossel
Production: Kim Richardson
Contributor: Kathryn Marshall

Maps produced by Oxford Cartographers, England.
Banknotes from Thomas Cook Currency Services.
Stamps from Stanley Gibbons.

Editorial Consultant: Andrew Gutelle
Guide to Kenya is approved by Kenya Tourist Office, London
Kenya Consultant: Macharia Mugo, The Council for the Promotion of Children's Science Publications
                in Africa; Nairobi
Managing Editor, Highlights New Products: Margie Hayes Richmond